T0062332

ALL THE PLACES

ALL THE PLACES

POEMS BY

MUSAWENKOSI KHANYILE

UHLANGA

2019

Zamo, my brother,
where in the universe does hard work ever go unrewarded?

———————————

All The Places
© Musawenkosi Khanyile, 2019, all rights reserved

First published in Cape Town, South Africa by uHlanga in 2019
UHLANGAPRESS.CO.ZA

Distributed outside South Africa by the African Books Collective
AFRICANBOOKSCOLLECTIVE.COM

ISBN: 978-0-620-83871-9

Edited by Nick Mulgrew
Cover photograph, design and typesetting by Nick Mulgrew

The body text of this book is set in Garamond Premier Pro 11PT on 15PT

ACKNOWLEDGEMENTS

The original version of *All The Places* was written as part of my thesis for my Masters in Creative Writing at the University of the Western Cape. I am eternally grateful to Kobus Moolman for being more than a supervisor.

I am grateful to the editors of the following publications in which earlier versions of some of the poems in this collection have appeared: *Five Points*, *Cutting Carrots the Wrong Way* (uHlanga/University of the Western Cape, 2017), *New Coin*, *New Contrast*, *Kalahari Review*, and *The Sol Plaatje European Union Poetry Anthology*.

Some of these poems appear in my chapbook entitled *The Internal Saboteur*, published by the African Poetry Book Fund in collaboration with Akashic Books as part of the *New-Generation African Poets Boxset*. My deepest gratitude goes to the editors, Kwame Dawes and Chris Abani.

Nick, my brother, thank you.

— M.K.

CONTENTS

RURAL

TOWNSHIP

URBAN

RURAL

A school visit

I remember how the drizzle came when I least expected it.
Even the sun was caught off-guard because it didn't move.
The heat rose from the pores of the soil when the drops fell,
and children in school uniform ran for shelter.

I was introduced, class by class, as an important guest.
I tried to put on the face of someone who has figured out this life thing,
attempting the walk of those who know where their lives are going.

Every class had a window with a hole in it,
a broken desk,
and something wrong with the door.

In the class without a door, I took the exercise book of a little girl
who smelled of paraffin and looked at the tree she had drawn –
a leafless tree with no bird in it.

She had a beautiful smile with a missing tooth.
She said *Doctor*, spitting out saliva,
when I asked her what she wanted to be when she grew up.

Habeni

You learn to tell the direction of the wind
during your walks by the side of the gravel road,

and that streams are running taps
where a cow and a boy might come to drink at the same time.

You also learn that a girl's hips are a good resting place for your hands,
and that kissing her for a long time by the river leaves you with memories

that remain long after she is no more,
shoved against a wall by an angry boyfriend years later,
to die in a government hospital.

And since her name was Nomvula,
you remember that one day on the mountain you saw the rain coming

and outran it.
But nobody believed that you could outrun the rain.

Ndundulu

In Ndundulu, my father's birthplace,
you point your finger to where your neighbour lives.
Huts seem so small in the distance but you never feel alone.

When a cow falls in your kraal and the beer is brewed,
the neighbour takes off his hat as he steps into your yard.
Word always reaches him.

SOME MEMORIES

We acquired skills in those hills.
Drugged the bees with smoke and took away their honey.

We learned to herd cattle through the fog. To locate cows by
their hoof prints and milk them with our bare hands.

Rivers were our bathing spot.
Water ran between rocks to our cupped hands.

We were shining with Vaseline by the time girls arrived with buckets of water.
The best romantic gesture was to help them balance the buckets on their heads.

In the hills bravery separated boys from men.
Scars on the back of the head were a sign of cowardice.

Friendship stood on the other side of a fist or stick fight.

The older boys held a handful of soil between the two of you and asked:

Are you afraid of this one? If your opponent hit the hand from underneath, sending dirt into your face – it was time to fight.

Hide-and-seek

Gaps in the wall let in the light
that reflects as small circles inside the house.
Mornings start with a game of obliterating them:
a boy blocking the rings with his right hand
and the left one and the right one again
as they keep seeping through his hands.

During the day, he wears a red jersey
with cuffs like shredded paper
and uses holes in the wall as binoculars
during the game of hide-and-seek.
Peeping through the wall while counting to twenty,
he sees his friends on the other side of the hut

making their way to their hiding spots.

THE ZINC TOILET

I walk toward the stinking smell.
Flies break out at my arrival.
I am careful with my body weight,
holding my bum mid-air:
a skill mastered after several warnings
from the plank, by means of a cracking sound.

SOME BUILD HOUSES TO ESCAPE FROM

When the strong wind comes,
the candle loses its flame.
Brown grass falls from the rooftop like a wig.
Walls crack.
But instead of a voice shouting
Run inside the house!,
everyone runs outside for safety.

To Nquthu

On my way to Nquthu where love is calling me,
the taxi hums its way up the hills of Ndundulu,
passing markets where women make a living selling fruit.
Their breasts dance up and down whenever a car stops:
the share of profit relies on whoever arrives first.

Before we leave Mpangeni, a woman stops to sell us ice cream.
The hurt in her eyes speaks of the many lives like hers
that are carried through days by little earnings.
At the end of each prayer reality awaits
where daily bread is not given, but sweated for.

We drive past a girl grappling with a water pump
and cows eating grass behind mud houses.
I know houses like these that are eaten away by heavy rains
and have fingerprints left on their walls
by the hands that built them.

My leg is sore by the time we reach Nquthu,
a town with only one set of traffic lights.
A boy holding a live chicken by its legs crosses the road.
I'm now thinking of all the lengths I will go to
for love.

Song in my heart

My girlfriend and I fight because I haven't yet mastered
the art of bathing in a dish.
Water spills all over the floor when I reach for my armpits.

She complains that I complain about this tiny room
where we hear kettles boiling next door
and neighbours yawning as they wake up.

But I always return to drown our love-making with uKhozi FM.
It takes me three hours on a taxi to get to her.
The song in my heart keeps me company.

BACK FROM THE TOWNSHIP

The houses are arranged like carriages.
A thrown stone falls into the neighbour's yard.
There's a pattern there. A straight line.

Here, our homes are disjointed,
and our roads take the shape of our dreams:
winding and not promising any destination.

There, I played in the streets.
Kicked the ball with friends on the tar road.
Played for hours until the street lights came on.
Then went and took a shower when I was done.
The water fell on my head like raindrops.

Here, I have to kneel over a zinc basin
and scoop up the water with my hands.

TOWNSHIP

FIND THE TRUTH

For Zamo

You know what it was like.
I left you the dining room floor
and graduated to a bed
after our sister left for varsity.
You know the roughness of our hands
and the fierceness of the sun.
You took the wheelbarrow from me
when you were strong enough
to fetch the crates of cold drinks
for our little family business,
all the way to the taxi rank and the salon
where our mother played stokvel.

What I want you to know now
is that there isn't much truth
in the township.
It crumbles like bread on the table.
In schools, children smile for a forty percent,
and success is a Golf GTI
parked next to a tiny house.
Brothers measure their success in whiskey bottles
and brush their big bellies in taverns.
Sisters fall in love with front seats
and wear off in the streets like car tyres.
You know what the township is like.

It's a victory to rise above all this;
to survive the streets that gush out blood
and open up into graves;
and even more to move out of the township
to places where mornings come with a sea breeze,
where people do not live in the smell of poverty.
Poverty has filled our nostrils.
We know the stench of unflushable toilets
and shacks that tell the tale of a man's suffering.
Do not forget the privilege
of having been close enough:
a man can only run away from what he knows.

Find the truth.
Do not forget our dining room floor,
and don't you dare drive a car
that's worth more than where you sleep.

MOTHER

You used to say what we have was because of you.
I did not understand, because you never worked anywhere else
but in the house.
You only buttered bread, never bought it.
But now that you live away from us, I see what you meant.
The house here is falling apart.
Even the kitchen door broke.
Dad put in five nails on the side to keep it locked at night.
I throw a used teabag through the broken window
by the kitchen sink where the air comes smashing
against the curtain on windy days.
None of this has moved dad yet.
He still walks in with his dirty sandals all the way to his bedroom.
I place a bucket there when it rains.
Holes in roofs beckon one another like shacks do outside the township:
there used to be a single hole there – now there are three.
I push dad's bed to the far right for the raindrops to miss it,
and place another bucket in the middle of the room.
But there's more than the falling apart going on here.

> Even the curtains miss your touch.
> Their dullness whispers this to me.

THE SOUND OF THE RAIN

The sound of the rain wakes me up in the middle of the night.
Or is it the sound coming from your room,
your bed squeaking and the drops hitting against the basin?
You have moved your bed such that it's now misaligned with the headboard.
The mop rests next to where you've been busy drying up after the rain.
In this house the rain doesn't quit on the rooftop.
It lands on the bed, and then after someone's labour, finds the basin.
You are here tonight, so it is your turn to move your bed.
My turn is when you are away on a job
that has still not rescued us from leaking roofs,
even though your long-service certificates are fading
inside the wall unit.

Known holes

My elbows sticking out of a school jersey.

Moisture inside my Toughees.

Toes peeping out of grey socks.

Cold air coming in through a window.

My last-option underwear.

My patched-up trousers.

The towel that shied away from the washing-line.

Tiny rooms with crawling things in the walls.

A leaking roof in my father's bedroom.

A bucket on standby for raindrops to fall into.

The outside toilet

The toilet is a walk away from our four-room house.
At night, I glance in all directions,
mindful of things that crawl in the dark.
I hold the weight of the door with my thigh
until it can stand on its own,
and inspect all the holes in the wall
before placing my bum on the seat.

His torn towel

There's not much of it left now.
His hands push through to the other side
when he grabs it.
He has mastered the art of folding it
until the holes fill in themselves.
He can't forget the day he came to the washing line

at the exact same time as the beautiful girl next door
who hung two towels opposite him
(one for her face and another for her body),
and looked at his with a wicked smile.
He no longer hangs his towel outside,
for fear of what her eyes will say.

First visit from a girl

The day before she visits, I turn over the mattress,
run my hand all over to check there are no spikes on this side.
The plan is to keep the curtains drawn in the kitchen,
to hide the huge hole in the window.
Nothing can be done about the coffee table,
which my younger brother calls a "convertible"
because of the top that comes off when he flips it
over the couch every night to make room to sleep.
Anyway, a man who hides everything is suspicious,
so I will let her see what cannot be hidden.
Tomorrow there'll be a smell of lavender on these tiles.

Nseleni

What a coincidence that my township is divided into wards,
that our homes stand one beside the other like hospital beds,
that so many of us die here,
that the goal is to make it out alive.

Nyanga

Healer
On the internet they say there's no other place in the country
where people kill each other like this.
You hold your name as a disguise.

Moon
I guess no one stands here long enough to look at the night sky.
Everyone's in a hurry to get behind a locked door.
Each night someone holds death in their hands.

Month
If we divide the number of murders by twelve
and give each month its equal share,
how many coffins does each one get?

WHAT THE TOWNSHIP DID TO US

My neighbour, stabbed in the neck with a knife,
died wearing his white All-Stars,
his body covered with a blanket outside the bar.
The girl with a round face, my first crush,
who thought her beauty would see her out of the township,
now avoids my eyes in the supermarket
that always runs out of plastic bags.

On a Thursday afternoon at the taxi rank,
I hear a familiar voice calling out a cheat
within a circle of men bent over dice.
When he – this guy I once shared a desk with – looks up,
I immediately throw my eyes away,
afraid to see what the township has done to him.

This tavern

In this tavern there are men with potbellies
who dish out advice they never use;
who bend too close while speaking gibberish,
their breath smelling like broken homes,
and their lips burned by years of bad habits.
You listen to them because respect dictates it,
and buy them a cigarette to get them off your back.

This tavern shelters lives that amount to nothing.
Dropouts find their solace here,
asking you to add R5 so they can have a quart.
Girls spread their legs for a cider
and squash themselves between married men,
who arrive home long after the pots have gone cold.
Empty bottles sleep sideways on the ground.

At this tavern

Our friend runs to hide when he sees her approaching,
almost knocking over the Hennessey he just bought.

She gathers her breath before she greets us and asks:
Where is Thami? Have you guys seen him?

Our loyalty answers:
No. Not today.

The frustration is clear on her face:
Eish, OK. Please tell him I came looking for him here.

He's not answering my calls.
It's about his son. He has nothing to eat.

Routines

The bed stands on bricks.
The bed moans without sex.
The fridge hums throughout the night.
The fridge no longer lights up when its door opens.
The son sleeps in the sitting room.
The son steals food when snores fill up the house.
The old wedding photo hangs on the wrinkled wall.
The cardboard stands in windows where glass used to be.
The torn towel swings on the washing line.
The mother fetches the bucket from outside near the decaying toilet.
The youngest sister pees inside the bucket at night.
The older sister empties it in the morning.
The mother prepares the lunchboxes.
The father rises and goes to work.

Improvisations

A brick to keep the door ajar.

An old cloth underneath the door to block out the cold.

Plastic hissing on the window fending off raindrops.

A car tyre on the roof to keep lightning at bay.

An old TV in the lounge needing to be tapped back to life.

The bed balancing on bricks.

Toothbrushes inside an old ice-cream container.

School socks drying behind the fridge.

Everything having to be reused before disposed.

Everything.

FORKS AND KNIVES

I don't know of any household
that uses forks and knives.
Every piece of food finds its way
to our mouths by spoon.
Our stomachs are beggars;
details do not matter
when we respond to their pleas.

Tuesday Morning

The woman crosses the street pushing a wheelbarrow,
heading towards the clinic.
In the wheelbarrow lies a boy with a grey blanket up to his neck,
his right arm dangling over the side.
The taxi coughs out dark smoke on a speed hump,
the driver removes his elbow from the window,
people stare,
the woman next to me stops chewing her sweetcorn.
We look for trails of blood on the street and find none.
Those close enough must see where tears are falling to the ground
from the woman's eyes.

URBAN

Outside KFC

He cannot escape the cracking voice
of a boy with a thin arm stretched out to him
outside KFC,
who eyes the brown packet in his hand
and begs:
Please, bhuti, please.

TO THE BUS STOP

It is drizzling. And I am walking next to a woman who drew our future with her finger on my chest last night. She is holding a small umbrella beneath which only she can fit. She has been calling me to join her, willing to sacrifice half of herself to the wetness. I refuse. Just before we come to the mall, a white Audi A3 lowers its speed to match ours. A young man in the passenger seat, holding a dumpy, calls for her attention. He is asking to talk to her. Asking for her number. Complimenting her legs. I stare at him to assure him that I exist. He keeps trying to talk to her, unaffected by my cold eyes. I keep my words inside me. I tell myself it will soon be over. He gives up. The car speeds off and disappears around the corner. I point ahead to the bus stop and tell my woman our bus has arrived.

TERMINATION

Something was made when we made love,
something we were not ready for.
So you called, panicking, telling me about the test,
asking that we meet.
I rose from the bed and put on my jacket,
my heart coming out of my mouth.

It would take only two days after this to find myself waiting for you:
Paterson Street, Newcastle, in broad daylight.
Two women, one pregnant, crossed the street as if to remind me,
God sees everything.

Before this we were on the road.
You said I was a mess, but you would marry me.
And I remembered that I had loved you since childhood.
You would be more than an hour inside the surgery.
And I would keep the engine running the whole time,
like a man ready to take off after a crime.

THE IMMACULATE TOILET

It smells like lavender here.
The floor is immaculate. The walls white.
I take a pee, push the button in the middle
and watch the yellow liquid disappear.
In the mirror I stare back at myself.
No rush. No smell to escape from.
I could eat in here.

To Cape Town

On a plane to Cape Town sitting by the window,
he sees clouds blanketing mountains.
Down there the roads are small
like pathways between tiles on the floor,
like lines on the trimmed head of a black boy.

UCT finally opened its doors and said to him:
Come on in.
Perhaps the boy in him who ran the yards of township schools,
and collected degrees from a rural university,
needed validation from UCT,

the brightest light beckoning dark moths,
to burn them out.

UCT

It's not about his blackness

that he is mistaken for a patient while standing outside the staff entrance
in the second week of his new job at UCT.
The white woman who asks him if he has an appointment with a psychologist
was on leave when he assumed his duties last week –
that's what it's about. Her meeting him for the first time
and not knowing who he is.

So, when he arrives in Hout Bay later that day
with the urge to get a six-pack of Hunters Gold,
and finds in the liquor store a white girl promoting some product,
and asks her where he can find a six-pack,
to which she blushingly responds that she doesn't work there,
it's not because he wanted to make one of them feel
what he feels almost every day.

It's not an act of vengeance.

MOWBRAY

After twenty-one days of moving from one B&B to another,
he is finally handed the keys to his flat: a two-bedroom apartment
in Station Road smelling of paint. After moving his bags inside
and gathering his breath, he looks around the space:

Rooms stripped of furniture. Empty rooms like himself,
like the people who come to talk to him all day,
patients who sit next to him and tell him how empty they feel.
How many times has he wondered what emptiness looks like?

For two nights he sleeps in the flat without curtains
and feels exposed in the morning when darkness can no longer hide him.
At work, he hides everything relentlessly,
especially when he sits crossing his legs, wearing a white shirt,

giving an occasional *Mmm* here and there,
pretending to know what fills up a hollow heart.

EMPTINESS

He worries too much, that's his problem.

Worries about silly things.

Even about his English which runs out like airtime while he speaks.

He's ashamed of everything,

including the master's degree that he obtained from a rural university

which sits at the bottom of the list.

Now he's at a top university where they needed the colour of his skin

to push their agenda of transformation.

But he likes it here. It's the opposite of where he's been.

He likes the office they gave him as well, which comes with a view of the mountain

and the highway. The highway is always busy.

He wonders where people go, where suffering cannot find them.

He's been battling with emptiness lately –

emptiness that awaits him in the flat that only has a bed and a barstool.

These days only thoughts keep him company. There's no one to talk to.

On his birthday his phone never rang

and he came close to calling his ex-girlfriend who had told him that he would end up alone,

but he stopped because he didn't know which word would come out first

between *bitch* and *witch*.

He doesn't want to fight anymore.

He wants peace. Only wants to fill up his heart –

to find someone willing to jump in where his heart keeps its mouth open.

The world opens up

For Zamo

The world opens up like a flower, but much more beautifully.
I am telling you this because the township walled us in.

In the township you carve your way out
like a prisoner committed to an escape plan.

I'm on this side of the rainbow now,
where the world is generous with itself.

Sometimes I go to the beach and wonder why waves calm me
at their most aggressive.

What are the side effects of surviving the township?
Why do I dream of someone plunging a knife into my chest?

I take nothing for granted. Even this bed.
This full fridge. This breath.

Once there was a bed with bricks for legs.
Once there was a hole in the underwear.

I remind myself of such things to remain humble.
I don't forget to live.

In the lift I startle strangers by merely greeting them.
Will hard work not level the ground for us?

I sit at the table with people who don't know leaking roofs
and the waiter hands each of us the same menu.

From my office window I see cars speeding on the highway
and think how awesome it would be, brother,

to drive with our arms stretched out like wings,
the air fanning us,

brushing against our black skin –
who would tell that I left you a dining room floor to sleep on?

BANTRY BAY

He doesn't know what comes over him
while standing on the balcony
of his room at the guesthouse.
He does not know, for example, why he cries
so suddenly while looking at the sea.
Why all this sentimentality about what's not his?
The sea is not his. This balcony is not his.
All that he has is himself –
when does he cry about that?

CAMPS BAY

We drove up the road in a rented Fiesta,
leaving Camps Bay behind us.

I had found a backroom where the rich live, and couldn't sleep alone.
You asked me to pull up at the side of the road

so I could take pictures of you with the mountain in the background,
even though you, unlike me, grew up in this city.

I said, *Imagine being stunned by the beauty of a lover like this,*
twenty years later.

You smiled and said, *Don't be a poet now,*
pulling me close enough to feel your nipples pressing against my chest –

even though you, unlike me, were somebody's fiancée.

Reporting from Cape Town

The newspaper article says toilets are overflowing in Khayelitsha
and people have nowhere to defecate.
The image of blue plastic toilets in a straight line is pasted on top.

Two students are brought to my office for therapy
after being robbed at gunpoint while waiting for the robot to turn green.

Clothes hang like lynched bodies over balconies in Nyanga.
In daylight nothing speaks of murder other than this.
Nothing else gives you a warning.

Shacks do not give one another enough space to breathe.
When one catches fire, thousands of people are left homeless.

In a restaurant in Milnerton, I am the only black customer.
I say to the black waitress, *Please come join me.*
She smiles to say she understands but lingers wherever she disappears to.

On a Saturday evening there is alcohol and meat and music in the township.
My people drink themselves to forgetfulness.

All the places

All the places he goes to
remind him of where he comes from.
He cannot escape his background; it's always with him.
Like now, seated at a long shiny table in a hotel
with colleagues who overlook his township English
and laugh kindly at his jokes.
He cannot look at his sparkling fork and knife
without thinking of holidays spent at his father's birthplace
gathered around a huge bowl of maas with his cousins,
digging in with his hands.

When you finally make it to the boardroom

Speak of growing up in the township as if it was an achievement.

Say that it was because you made it out alive.

Tell them you come from a place that chewed you up and spat you out when it thought it was done with you.

Correct those who ask you: *What was it like growing up in the township?*

Say the appropriate question is: *How did you survive the township?*

Tell them the township swallowed many of your peers.

Close your eyes for a second,

count the names of those you knew who got stabbed or arrested,

steady yourself when you come to the total.

Wall in the tears. Keep tears to yourself.

Talk about a mother who prayed for you on your way to school,

looking at you through a broken window.

Talk about a father who taught you how to balance your bed on bricks.

Think of those from the same block who amounted to nothing.

Think of street corners where bodies lay bloodied and cold.

Be the first one to say: *None of that matters anymore.*

Gobble down a glass of water.

Move onto another topic.

POETRY FOR THE PEOPLE | UHLANGAPRESS.CO.ZA

—— ALSO AVAILABLE ——

In a Free State and *Foundling's Island* by P.R. Anderson

White Blight by Athena Farrokhzad, translated by Jennifer Hayashida
IN ASSOCIATION WITH ARGOS BOOKS, USA

Zikr by Saaleha Idrees Bamjee

Milk Fever by Megan Ross

Liminal by Douglas Reid Skinner

Collective Amnesia by Koleka Putuma
WINNER OF THE 2018 GLENNA LUSCHEI PRIZE FOR AFRICAN POETRY
CITY PRESS BOOK OF THE YEAR 2017

Thungachi by Francine Simon

Modern Rasputin by Rosa Lyster

Prunings by Helen Moffett
CO-WINNER OF THE 2017 SOUTH AFRICAN LITERARY AWARD FOR POETRY

Questions for the Sea by Stephen Symons
2017 GLENNA LUSCHEI PRIZE FOR AFRICAN POETRY HONOURABLE MENTION

Failing Maths and My Other Crimes by Thabo Jijana
WINNER OF THE 2016 INGRID JONKER PRIZE

Matric Rage by Genna Gardini
COMMENDED FOR THE 2016 INGRID JONKER PRIZE

the myth of this is that we're all in this together by Nick Mulgrew

—— AVAILABLE FROM OUR FRIENDS AT CRANE RIVER ——

The Mushroom Summer of Skipper Darling by Tony Voss

Voices from Another Room by Stuart Payne

AVAILABLE FROM GOOD BOOKSTORES IN SOUTH AFRICA *&* NAMIBIA
& FROM THE AFRICAN BOOKS COLLECTIVE ELSEWHERE

Printed in the United States
By Bookmasters